ENGLISH PREMIER QUIZ (1992-20~~)

300 FOOTBALL QUESTIONS ON PLAYER RECORDS,
STATISTICS, TRANSFERS, TROPHIES & LOTS MORE TO
TEST YOUR KNOWLEDGE

By
QuizGuy

Preface

"I respect the Premier League."

Zlatan Ibrahimovic

"The Premier League is a championship that amazes me."

Neymar Jr.

"The Premier League is the place to be"

David Silva

"The Premier League is in my heart."

Dimitar Berbatov

The English Premier League is into its 28th season and it has provided us with plenty of entertainment, controversies and memorable moments over the years. The EPL is thought of by many as the greatest league in the world for a variety of reasons. One of those reasons being the talented players from home and abroad who we have had the pleasure of watching over the years.

The English Premier League Quiz (1992-2020) is engaging and informative and will provide hours of entertainment for all of those who love The English Premier League. Hopefully the quiz will remind you of some of your heroes and of some forgotten talents over the years.

QuizGuy has designed a quiz to test your knowledge on the players we have watched and marveled at since the beginning of The English Premier League. The quiz consists of 20 rounds each made up of 15 questions. The beginning of the book has easier questions and gradually the questions will get more difficult as the rounds pass by. You will be tested on lots of different topics related to player records, statistics, transfers, trophies and lots more.

Now it the time to put your knowledge to the test! Good Luck!

CONTENTS

Round 1

1. Which player was suspended for 11 games after pushing over referee Paul Alcock in September 1998?

2. Which Colombian striker signed for Aston Villa from River Plate for £9.5 million in January 2001?

3. Who has scored the most goals in the English Premier League?

4. Who is the most expensive player to be signed by a Premier League club?

5. Which team did Frank Lampard move to from West Ham in June 2001?

6. Which player assisted Sergio Aguero's injury time title winning goal against QPR in the 2011-2012 season?

7. Which Australian player has the scored the most Premier League goals?

8. Which player holds the record for the most appearances in the Premier League at 653 games?

9. Which player holds the record for the most consecutive Premier League games to have scored in? The record is for 11 consecutive games.

10. Which defender became Britain's most expensive transfer at the time by moving from Leeds United to Manchester United in July 2002?

11. Which two Newcastle United players were sent off for fighting each other in a game against Aston Villa?

12. Can you name the first Premier League club that Mohamed Salah signed for?

13. Which player received a 12-match ban for fighting with several Man City players on the last day of a Premier League season?

14. How old was Wayne Rooney when he transferred from Everton to Manchester United?

15. Which player has appeared in the most Premier League seasons? The player in question played across a record total of 22 seasons.

Round 1 Answers

1. Paulo Di Canio

2. Juan Pablo Angel

3. Alan Shearer

4. Paul Pogba

5. Chelsea

6. Mario Balotelli

7. Mark Viduka

8. Gareth Barry

9. Jamie Vardy

10. Rio Ferdinand

11. Lee Bowyer and Kieron Dyer

12. Chelsea

13. Joey Barton

14. 18 years old

15. Ryan Giggs

Round 2

16. Who was the first goalkeeper to score a goal in the Premier League?

17. Who is the only Uruguayan player to win the Golden Boot?

18. Which club did Carlos Tevez make his Premier League debut for?

19. Which club did Les Ferdinand play for first in the Premier League?

20. Which South African player captained Leeds United?

21. Who moved from Marseille to Chelsea for a transfer fee of £24 million in July 2004?

22. How many times has Sergio Aguero won the Golden Boot?

23. A player scored the fastest Premier League hat-trick in 2 minutes and 56 seconds. Can you name the player?

24. Which player has scored the most penalties in the Premier League?

25. Which player has scored the most Premier League goals in his debut season?

26. Which player has received the most yellow cards? The record stands at 123 yellow cards.

27. Which player has assisted the most goals in consecutive games? The record stands at 7 games with an assist.

28. One player has scored a record 3 hat-tricks against the same club. Can you name the player? The club that the hat-tricks were scored against was Norwich City.

29. Who is the oldest ever player to score a goal in the Premier League? The player scored this goal at 40 years and 268 days.

30. Who are the only two players to have scored Premier League penalties with both feet?

Round 2 Answers

16.   Peter Schmeichel

17.   Luis Suarez

18.   West Ham

19.   QPR

20.   Lucas Radebe

21.   Didier Drogba

22.   One time

23.   Sadio Mane

24.   Alan Shearer

25.   Kevin Phillips

26.   Gareth Barry

27.   Mesut Ozil

28.   Luis Suarez

29.   Teddy Sheringham

30.   Bobby Zamora and Obafemi Martins

Round 3

31. Which two players have missed the most penalties in the Premier League? They have both missed a total of 11 penalties.

32. Who captained Leicester City's title winning season in 2015/2016?

33. One player has scored a record 39 Premier League goals in a calendar year. Can you name the player?

34. Which Argentinian player broke British transfer records, costing a Premier League club £28.1 million in July 2001?

35. Which Ukrainian player broke British transfer records, costing a Premier League club £30.8 million in July 2006?

36. One player has scored a record of 12 hat-tricks in the Premier League. Can you name the player?

37. Who is the most substituted player in Premier League history? He was substituted in a record of 134 games.

38. Who is the player to have scored the most headed goals in the Premier League?

39. One player scored a record 9 headers in one single Premier League season. Can you name the player?

40. One player assisted a record of 20 goals in one single Premier League season. Can you name the player?

41. Who is the only Republic of Ireland international to have scored more than 100 goals in the Premier League?

42. Who is the highest scoring midfielder in Premier League history, with a record of 177 goals?

43. Who is the highest scoring defender in Premier League history, with a record of 41 goals?

44. One defender scored 22 penalties which is a record for a Premier League defender. Can you name the player?

45. Who are the only two Netherlands' internationals to have scored over 100 goals in the Premier League?

Round 3 Answers

31. Alan Shearer and Wayne Rooney

32. Wes Morgan

33. Harry Kane

34. Juan Sebastian Veron

35. Andriy Shevchenko

36. Sergio Aguero

37. Ryan Giggs

38. Peter Crouch

39. Duncan Ferguson

40. Thierry Henry

41. Robbie Keane

42. Frank Lampard

43. John Terry

44. David Unsworth

45. Robin Van Persie and Jimmy Floyd Hasselbaink

Round 4

46. Who are the only two French players to have scored over 100 Premier League goals?

47. Who is the only Armenian player to have made appearances in the Premier League?

48. Who is the only player from Kenya to have played in the Premier League?

49. Who is the youngest ever player to have made a hat-trick of assists? He did this against Watford at the age of 20 years and 143 days.

50. One player has a record 13 Premier League winners' medals. Can you name the player?

51. One player scored a record 10 Premier League goals in a calendar month. Can you name the player?

52. Who is the only player to score 30 goals or more in three consecutive seasons?

53. Can you name the five players that have scored 5 goals in a single game?

54. One player holds a record of scoring 183 goals for one single Premier League club. Can you name the player?

55. Who is the only Portuguese player to win the Golden Boot?

56. Who are the only two players to have scored over 100 Premier League goals, without any of them goals being scored from the penalty spot?

57. Which player has scored the most goals for Liverpool in the Premier League?

58. Which player has scored the most goals for Tottenham Hotspur in the Premier League?

59. Who is Everton´s record buy?

60. Which Spanish player has provided the most assists in the Premier League?

Round 4 Answers

46. Thierry Henry and Nicolas Anelka

47. Henrikh Mkhitaryan

48. Victor Wanyama

49. Trent Alexander-Arnold

50. Ryan Giggs

51. Luis Suarez

52. Alan Shearer

53. Jermaine Defoe, Andrew Cole, Sergio Agüero, Alan Shearer and Dimitar Berbatov

54. Wayne Rooney

55. Cristiano Ronaldo

56. Emile Heskey and Les Ferdinand

57. Robbie Fowler

58. Harry Kane

59. Gylfi Sigurdsson

60. Cesc Fabregas

Round 5

61. Who is the Netherlands international that has provided the most assists in the Premier League?

62. Who is the top scoring Togolese international in Premier League history?

63. Only one non-British player has made over 500 appearances in the Premier League. He is a goalkeeper. Can you name him?

64. Which non-British outfield player has made the most appearances in the Premier League? He is a defender and he is from France.

65. Which player has scored the most Premier League goals for Everton?

66. Which Premier League club did Dwight Yorke score the most goals for?

67. Which player has scored the most goals for Aston Villa in the Premier League?

68. Which Argentinian player has made the most appearances in the Premier League?

69. Which Peruvian player has made the most appearances in the Premier League?

70. Which Premier League club did Netherlands international Bryan Roy play for?

71. Who is Norwich City's record Premier League goal scorer with 33 goals?

72. Who is West Bromwich Albion´s record Premier League goal scorer with 30 goals?

73. Which Premier League club did Stan Collymore score the most league goals for?

74. Which player has made the most Premier League appearances for Leeds United? He made a record of 325 appearances.

75. Which player has made the most Premier League appearances for Arsenal? He made a record of 333 appearances.

Round 5 Answers

61. Dennis Bergkamp

62. Emmanuel Adebayor

63. Mark Schwarzer

64. Sylvain Distin

65. Romelu Lukaku

66. Aston Villa

67. Gabriel Agbonlahor

68. Pablo Zabaleta

69. Nolberto Solano

70. Nottingham Forest

71. Chris Sutton

72. Peter Odemwingie

73. Nottingham Forest

74. Gary Kelly

75. Ray Parlour

Round 6

76. Who is the Argentinian player that was signed for the most money by a Premier League club?

77. Who is the U.S.A. player that was signed for the most money by a Premier League club?

78. A Colombian player was signed for £42 million by a Premier League club. This is the most a club has paid for a Colombian player. Can you name him?

79. How much was the transfer fee for Sol Campbell's move from Tottenham Hotspur to Arsenal?

80. Where did Manchester United sign Eric Cantona from?

81. Hernan Jorge Crespo signed for Chelsea in August 2003 for £16.8 million. Which club sold him?

82. Which club sold Cristiano Ronaldo to Manchester United?

83. Where did Arsenal sign Sylvain Wiltord from for £13 million?

84. Which Ivorian was signed by Swansea City for £12 million from Vitesse?

85. Which Italian club did Chelsea sign Gianfranco Zola from for £4.5 million in November 1996?

86. Which Brazilian signed for Middlesbrough for £4.75 million in October 1995?

87. Which Netherlands international did Manchester United sign from PSV in the summer of 1998?

88. Which team did Arsenal sign Dennis Bergkamp from?

89. Which Premier League club did Michael Ballack join on a free transfer from Bayern Munich?

90. Which Brazilian did Manchester City sign on deadline day from Real Madrid for £32.5 million on 1st September 2008?

Round 6 Answers

76.   Angel Di Maria

77.   Christian Pulisic

78.   Davison Sanchez

79.   Free transfer

80.   Leeds United

81.   Inter Milan

82.   Sporting Lisbon

83.   Bordeaux

84.   Wilfried Bony

85.   Parma

86.   Juninho

87.   Jaap Stam

88.   Inter Milan

89.   Chelsea

90.   Robinho

Round 7

91. How many Premier League titles did Paul Ince win in his career?

92. How many times did Ruud van Nistelrooy win the Golden Boot?

93. Gary Speed made a total of 535 appearances in the Premier League. How many teams did he play for in the Premier League?

94. How many teams did current England Manager Gareth Southgate play for in the Premier League?

95. How many Premier League titles did Nicolas Anelka win in his career?

96. How many times did Ivorian striker Didier Drogba win the golden boot?

97. How old was Theo Walcott when he signed for Arsenal from Southampton?

98. How many Premier League clubs did Djibril Cisse play for?

99. How many seasons in total did Jurgen Klinsmann play in the Premier League?

100. How many times did Thierry Henry win the Golden Boot?

101. How many times did Harry Redknapp sign Niko Kranjcar?

102. How many times did Jose Mourinho sign Nemanja Matic?

103. How many Premier League clubs did Nwankwo Kanu play for?

104. How many Premier League titles did John Terry win with Chelsea?

105. How many Premier League clubs did Dimitar Berbatov play for?

Round 7 Answers

91. Two

92. One

93. Four

94. Three

95. Two

96. Two

97. 16 years old

98. Three

99. Two

100. Four

101. Three

102. Two

103. Three

104. Five

105. Three

Round 8

106. Which former Arsenal player admitted he was responsible for throwing a slice of pizza which hit Sir Alex Ferguson in the face? This happened in the tunnel after Manchester United had ended Arsenal's long unbeaten run in October 2004.

107. Which player received a 9 month ban from football after doing a flying kick at a fan in the crowd? The player in question had already been red carded in the game.

108. How many matches was Luis Suarez banned for when he bit Branislav Ivanovic on the arm?

109. Roy Keane did a knee-high foul on a Manchester City player and received a red card for this incident in a 2001 Manchester derby. Can you name the player he fouled?

110. Which player scored from his own half on the opening day of the 1996/1997 season?

111. A Steven Gerrard slip proved costly for Liverpool's title challenge in the 2013-2014 season. Can you name the Chelsea player that went on to score after Gerrard's slip?

112. Which Stoke City player scored from his own half at Stamford Bridge?

113. Which Manchester United player was sent off in their 4-1 home defeat to Liverpool in March 2009?

114. Which player scored from his own half against Newcastle United for Liverpool? The game was in September 2006.

115. Which Manchester City player scored against his former club Arsenal and ran the length of the pitch to celebrate in front of his former team's fans?

116. Wayne Rooney was arguing with a referee and went on to score an amazing volley a few seconds later for Manchester United. Which team did he score against?

117. Who is the only Welsh player to win the PFA Players' Player of the Year award two times?

118. Which Manchester City player scored a crucial goal from outside the box to secure an important 1-0 victory over Leicester City on 6th May 2019? This helped Manchester City to win the title six days later.

119. Who was the player that crossed the ball for Wayne Rooney's famous overhead kick which won the Manchester Derby in February 2011? The game finished 2-1 to Manchester United. The player that assisted Rooney's goal also scored Manchester United's first goal of the game.

120. How many times did Cristiano Ronaldo win the PFA Players' Player of the Year award?

Round 8 Answers

106.	Cesc Fabregas
107.	Eric Cantona
108.	10 matches
109.	Alf-Inge Haland
110.	David Beckham
111.	Demba Ba
112.	Charlie Adam
113.	Nemanja Vidic
114.	Xabi Alonso
115.	Emmanuel Adebayor
116.	Newcastle United
117.	Gareth Bale
118.	Vincent Kompany
119.	Nani
120.	Two times

Round 9

121. Which club did Arsenal sign Cesc Fabregas from?

122. Riyad Mahrez was signed by Leicester City from a team in France. Can you name the club that sold him?

123. How many English Premier League clubs did David Ginola player for?

124. Manchester City signed a player from Hamburg that went on to captain the team and make over 250 appearances for the club. Can you name the player?

125. Mark Viduka is Leeds United's all-time leading goal scorer in the Premier League? Which team did Leeds United sign him from?

126. Who is Portsmouth's all-time leading goal scorer in the Premier League?

127. Which three Premier League clubs did Patrik Berger make appearances for?

128. Which Premier League club did Pierre van Hooijdonk play for?

129. Which two Premier League clubs did Georgian international Georgi Kinkladze play for?

130. Which player is Southampton's all-time leading scorer in the Premier League?

131. Which club did striker James Beattie make the most appearances for in the Premier League?

132. Which team did Chelsea sign Arjen Robben from for £12.1 million?

133. Which club did Damien Duff make the most appearances for in the Premier League?

134. Manchester United signed a left back from Monaco that went on to make over 250 league appearances for them and win 5 Premier League titles. Can you name the player?

135. Arsenal signed Patrick Vieira for £3.5 million in August 1996. Can you name the club that sold him to Arsenal?

Round 9 Answers

121. Barcelona

122. Le Havre

123. Four teams

124. Vincent Kompany

125. Celtic

126. Yakubu

127. Liverpool, Portsmouth and Aston Villa

128. Nottingham Forest

129. Manchester City and Derby County

130. Matt Le Tissier

131. Southampton

132. PSV

133. Fulham

134. Patrice Evra

135. AC Milan

Round 10

136. Which player has scored the most own goals in the Premier League out of Michael Duberry, Titus Bramble and Frank Sinclair?

137. Which player assisted more goals in the Premier League out of Steven Gerrard, David Beckham and Dennis Bergkamp?

138. Please name the goalkeeper that has kept the most clean sheets in the Premier League out of the following goalkeepers. Is it David Seaman, Edwin van der Sar or Peter Schmeichel?

139. Which defender has made the most appearances in the Premier League out of these defenders? Is it Rio Ferdinand, Jamie Carragher or Sol Campbell?

140. Which player has received the most red cards out of Joey Barton, Roy Keane and Nemanja Vidic?

141. Please name the player that received the most red cards in the Premier League out of Vinnie Jones, Martin Keown and Tony Adams?

142. Please name the player that won the most Premier League titles out of the following players. Is it David Beckham, John Terry or Yaya Toure?

143. Which player has scored the most Premier League goals out of Ruud van Nistlerooy, Jamie Vardy and Kevin Phillips?

144. Please name the player that has assisted the most Premier League goals out of Cesc Fabregas, Frank Lampard and Wayne Rooney?

145. Which player has won the most Premier League titles out of Didier Drogba, Thierry Henry and Carlos Tevez?

146. Which defender has scored the most Premier League goals in their career out of William Gallas, Sami Hyypia and Nemanja Vidic?

147. Please name the player that has won the most league titles out of the following players. Is it Alan Shearer, Eden Hazard or Cristiano Ronaldo?

148. Which player has scored the most Premier League goals out of Cristiano Ronaldo, Carlos Tevez and Fernando Torres?

149. Please name the player that has scored the most own goals in the Premier League. Is it Anton Ferdinand, Rio Ferdinand or Martin Skrtel?

150. Which player has scored the most Premier League goals out of Louis Saha, Ole Gunnar Solskjaer and Luis Suarez?

Round 10 Answers

136. Frank Sinclair

137. Dennis Bergkamp

138. David Seaman

139. Jamie Carragher

140. Roy Keane

141. Vinnie Jones

142. David Beckham

143. Jamie Vardy

144. Cesc Fabregas

145. Didier Drogba

146. William Gallas

147. Cristiano Ronaldo

148. Fernando Torres

149. Martin Skrtel

150. Ole Gunnar Solskjaer

Round 11

151. How many Premier League titles has Thibaut Courtois won?

152. How many times did Juninho sign on loan or permanently for Middlesbrough?

153. What was the squad number that Thierry Henry wore on his shirt for his whole first stint at Arsenal?

154. Which squad number did Frank Lampard wear on his shirt for his entire time at Chelsea?

155. Can you name the four Premier League clubs that Michael Owen played for?

156. Which squad number did Mario Balotelli wear for both Manchester City and Liverpool?

157. How many Premier League titles did Steve Bruce win?

158. Who are the two same Premier League teams that both Henning Berg and David May have played for?

159. Who are the two same Premier League teams that both Michael Duberry and Jimmy Floyd Hasselbaink have played for?

160. Which squad number did Dwight Yorke wear on his shirt at Manchester United?

161. Which squad number did Jamie Carragher wear for his entire career at Liverpool?

162. What was the squad number that John Terry wore at Chelsea for his entire time there?

163. What squad number was given to Cristiano Ronaldo when he signed for Manchester United?

164. Which squad number did Dennis Bergkamp wear on his shirt when he played at Arsenal?

165. What number did Tim Sherwood wear for Blackburn Rovers for his entire time at the club?

Round 11 Answers

151.   Two

152.   Three

153.   14

154.   8

155.   Liverpool, Newcastle United, Manchester United and Stoke City

156.   45

157.   Three

158.   Blackburn Rovers and Manchester United

159.   Chelsea and Leeds United

160.   19

161.   23

162.   26

163.   7

164.   10

165.   4

Round 12

166. Who are the only two players to win Premier League titles with both Manchester City and Arsenal?

167. Who is the only player to win Premier League titles with both Blackburn Rovers and Manchester United?

168. Who is the only South Korean player to have a Premier League winners medal?

169. Who is the only Mexican player to have a Premier League winners medal?

170. Two players have won Premier League titles with both Arsenal and Chelsea. Can you name the two players?

171. Only one Uruguayan player has a Premier League winners medal. Can you name the player?

172. Who is the only Italian player to have a Premier League winners medal?

173. Only one Icelandic player has a Premier League winners medal. Can you name him?

174. Who is the only player to win Premier League titles with both Leicester City and Manchester City?

175. Who are the only two players to win Premier League titles with both Chelsea and Leicester City?

176. Which Portuguese player has the most Premier League winners' medals?

177. Can you name the three Swedish players that have Premier League winners´ medals?

178. Only one Colombian has a Premier League winners medal. Can you name him?

179. Which Russian player has the most Premier League winners' medals?

180. Which Brazilian player has the most Premier League winners' medals?

Round 12 Answers

166.   Kolo Toure and Gael Clichy

167.   Henning Berg

168.   Park Ji-Sung

169.   Javier Hernandez

170.   Nicolas Anelka and Ashley Cole

171.   Diego Forlan

172.   Mario Balotelli

173.   Eidur Gudjohnsen

174.   Riyad Mahrez

175.   N´Golo Kante and Robert Huth

176.   Nani

177.   Freddie Ljungberg, Henrik Larsson and Jesper Blomqvist

178.   Juan Cuadrado

179.   Andrei Kanchelskis

180.   Anderson

Round 13

181. Only one player has won Premier League titles with both Manchester City and Manchester United. Can you name the player?

182. Only one Jamaican player has a Premier League winners medal. Can you name the player?

183. Who is the only Ecuadorian player to have a Premier League winners medal?

184. Which Scottish player has the most Premier League winners' medals?

185. Who are the two Republic of Ireland internationals that have won the Premier League the most times?

186. Who are the two Bosnia and Herzegovina internationals that have won the Premier League?

187. Only one Polish international has a Premier League winners medal. Can you name him?

188. Who is the only Bulgarian player to have a Premier League winners medal?

189. Two Cameroonian players have won the Premier League twice. Can you name the two players?

190. Two Northern Ireland Internationals have Premier League winners' medals. Can you name the two players?

191. Who are the two Japanese players to have Premier League winners´ medals?

192. Can you name the three Nigerian players that have Premier League winners´ medals?

193. Two father-son duos have won the Premier League. Can you name the two father-son duos?

194. Which Premier League defender has won the most Premier League titles?

195. Which Premier League striker has won the most Premier league titles?

Round 13 Answers

181. Carlos Tevez

182. Wes Morgan

183. Antonio Valencia

184. Darren Fletcher

185. Dennis Irwin and Roy Keane

186. Edin Dzeko and Asmir Begovic

187. Tomasz Kuszczak

188. Dimitar Berbatov

189. Lauren and Geremi

190. Jonny Evans and Roy Carroll

191. Shinji Kagawa and Shinji Okazaki

192. Nwankwo Kanu, Jon Obi Mikel and Victor Moses

193. Ian Wright/Shaun Wright-Phillips and Peter Schmeichel/Kasper Schmeichel

194. Gary Neville

195. Ole Gunnar Solskjaer

Round 14

196. Which two Premier League clubs did Romelu Lukaku player for on loan?

197. Carlos Tevez and Javier Mascerano joined West Ham in the summer of 2006. Can you name the club that sold the two players to West Ham?

198. Which World Cup winner joined Birmingham City on loan in 2003?

199. Which two Premier League teams has Daniel Sturridge played for on loan?

200. Robbie Keane was loaned out by Inter Milan to a Premier League club in December 2000. Can you name the Premier League club he joined on loan?

201. Which Spanish player did Everton sign on loan from Real Sociedad in January 2005?

202. Which Premier League team did George Weah sign for on loan in January 2000?

203. Real Madrid legend Fernando Hierro joined a Premier League club for the last year of his playing career. Which Premier League team did he join?

204. Jurgen Klinsmann joined Tottenham Hotspur for the second time during the 1997-1998 season. He signed on loan from an Italian team. Can you name the Italian team that loaned him to Tottenham Hotspur?

205. Jack Wilshere has played for two Premier League clubs on loan. Can you name the two teams?

206.   Ghanaian international Asamoah Gyan was signed by a Premier League club for £13 million from Rennes in August 2010. Which Premier League team signed him?

207.   Which Premier League club did Danny Welbeck join on loan in August 2010?

208.   Which two Premier League clubs has Colombian international Radamel Falcao played for on loan?

209.   Alexandre Pato signed for a Premier League club on loan in January 2016. Which Premier League club did he join on loan?

210.   Which Premier League club did Kyle Walker play for on loan?

Round 14 Answers

196.   West Bromwich Albion and Everton

197.   Corinthians

198.   Christophe Dugarry

199.   Bolton Wanderers and West Bromwich Albion

200.   Leeds United

201.   Mikel Arteta

202.   Chelsea

203.   Bolton Wanderers

204.   Sampdoria

205.   Bolton Wanderers and Bournemouth

206.   Sunderland

207.   Sunderland

208.   Manchester United and Chelsea

209.   Chelsea

210.   Aston Villa

Round 15

211.   Which Manchester United player scored the 25,000th goal in the Premier League?

212.   One Premier League goalkeeper kept a record 24 clean sheets in one season. Can you name the goalkeeper?

213.   Which player scored the first Premier League hat-trick?

214.   Who is the only player in Premier League history to join a club and win the title in his first season, then to transfer to another Premier League team and win the title in his second season?

215.   Which goalkeeper holds the record of 14 consecutive games without conceding a goal?

216.   Who are the two players to win the Golden Boot with one team and then successfully defend the Golden Boot after making a transfer to another club?

217.   Who are the only two players to have won the Ballon d´Or whilst playing for a Premier League team?

218.   Who are the two left sided midfielders that were never booked in their career? Both scored over 50 goals and played over 350 games.

219.   Who was the first outfield player to play every single minute of the season for a team that won the Premier League title that same season?

220.   Who is the player that has scored the most goals in a single game after coming on as a substitute? The player in question holds the record after coming on and scoring 4 goals.

221. Which Tottenham Hotspur player scored the 10,000th goal in the Premier League?

222. Which Blackburn Rovers player scored the 5,000th goal in the Premier League?

223. Who is the most expensive goalkeeper to be signed by a Premier League club?

224. Who is the most expensive defender to be signed by a Premier League club?

225. Who is the most expensive striker to be signed by a Premier League club?

Round 15 Answers

211. Zlatan Ibrahimovic

212. Petr Cech

213. Eric Cantona

214. N´Golo Kante

215. Edwin van der Sar

216. Alan Shearer and Robin van Persie

217. Michael Owen and Cristiano Ronaldo

218. Ryan Giggs and Damien Duff

219. Gary Pallister

220. Ole Gunnar Solskjaer

221. Les Ferdinand

222. Chris Sutton

223. Kepa Arrizabalaga

224. Harry Maguire

225. Romelu Lukaku

Round 16

226. Who is the player that was sold for the most amount of money by a Premier League club?

227. Which club did Manchester City sign Belgian international Kevin De Bruyne from?

228. Eden Hazard signed for Chelsea in June 2012. Which club did Chelsea sign him from?

229. Which club did Arsenal sign Robin van Persie from?

230. Virgil van Dijk´s first club in the Premier League was Southampton. Which team did Southampton sign the Netherlands international from?

231. Fernando Torres signed for Liverpool in July 2007. Which club did Liverpool sign him from?

232. In the summer of 2003, Chelsea signed Claude Makelele. Which team did Chelsea sign him from?

233. In June 1997, Emmanuel Petit signed for Arsenal. Which team did Arsenal sign him from?

234. Which club did Arsenal sign Robert Pires from?

235. In 1998, Chelsea signed Marcel Desailly. Can you name the team they signed him from?

236. Marc Overmars was part of the Arsenal team that won the Premier League in the 1997-1998 season. Which team did Arsenal sign him from?

237. David Ginola signed for Newcastle United in 1995. Which team did Newcastle United sign him from?

238. Xabi Alonso signed for Liverpool in August 2004. Which team did Liverpool sign him from?

239. In January 2011, Liverpool signed Luis Suarez. Can you name the team they signed him from?

240. Angel Di Maria played for Manchester United for just one season. What club did Manchester United sign him from?

Round 16 Answers

226. Philippe Coutinho

227. Wolfsburg

228. Lille

229. Feyenoord

230. Celtic

231. Atletico Madrid

232. Real Madrid

233. Monaco

234. Marseille

235. A.C. Milan

236. Ajax

237. Paris Saint-Germain

238. Real Sociedad

239. Ajax

240. Real Madrid

Round 17

241. Can you name the three players that played for Premier League clubs at the time, who played in the World Cup 1998 final?

242. Can you name the two Premier League players at the time who played and were on the winning team in the World Cup 2010 final?

243. Can you name the three Premier League players at the time who played and were on the winning team in the World Cup 2014 final?

244. Can you name the four Premier League players at the time who played and were on the winning team in the World Cup 2018 final?

245. Who was the Premier League player at the time who finished as the top goal scorer in Euro 2004?

246. Which Premier League striker finished as the top goal scorer in Euro 1996?

247. Who is the Finnish international that has made the most appearances in the Premier League for someone from that country? He made a total of 436 appearances.

248. Who is the player to make the most appearances in the Premier League that is from Denmark? He is a goalkeeper who made a total of 364 appearances.

249. Who is the top appearance maker from Germany in Premier League history?

250. Who is the top appearance maker from Norway in Premier League history? He made a total of 321 appearances.

251. Who is the top appearance maker from The Netherlands in the Premier League? He is a midfielder and made a total of 384 appearances.

252. Who is the top scoring Icelandic player in Premier League history?

253. Who is the top scoring Italian player in Premier League history?

254. Can you name the Costa Rican player that has scored the most goals for a player from Costa Rica in the Premier League?

255. Who is the top scoring Jamaican player in Premier League history?

Round 17 Answers

241. Frank Lebouf, Emmanuel Petit and Patrick Vieira

242. Cesc Fabregas and Fernando Torres

243. Mesut Ozil, Andre Schurrle and Per Mertesacker

244. Hugo Lloris, N´Golo Kante, Paul Pogba and Olivier Giroud

245. Milan Baros

246. Alan Shearer

247. Jussi Jaaskelainen

248. Thomas Sorensen

249. Robert Huth

250. John Arne Riise

251. George Boateng

252. Gylfi Sigurdsson

253. Paolo Di Canio

254. Paolo Wanchope

255. Jason Euell

Round 18

256. Can you name the two Premier League clubs that Ugo Ehiogu played for?

257. Who is the top scoring Malian international in Premier League history?

258. Norwegian international John Carew played for two teams in the Premier League? Can you name the two clubs?

259. Who is the top scoring Danish player in Premier League history?

260. Who is the top scoring German player in Premier League history?

261. Goalkeeper Nigel Martyn made 372 appearances in the Premier League. He played for three different teams. Which teams did he play for?

262. Can you name the Croatian player that has scored the most goals in the Premier League?

263. Who is the top scoring Finnish player in Premier League history?

264. Kevin Davies made 444 appearances in the Premier League. He played for three different teams. Can you name the teams he played for?

265. Can you name the three teams that Stephen Carr played for in the Premier League?

266. Joe Cole made a total of 378 appearances in the Premier League. Can you name the four teams that he played for?

267. Who is the only Serbian to have scored a hat-trick in the Premier League?

268. Only one Israeli player has ever scored a hat-trick in the Premier League. Can you name the player?

269. Can you name the four players that have scored a hat-trick in the Premier League and still ended up on the losing side in that game?

270. Can you name the player that scored the first perfect hat-trick in the Premier League?

Round 18 Answers

256. Aston Villa and Middlesbrough

257. Frederic Kanoute

258. Aston Villa and Stoke City

259. Christian Eriksen

260. Mesut Ozil

261. Crystal Palace, Leeds United and Everton

262. Nikica Jelavic

263. Mikael Forssell

264. Blackburn Rovers, Southampton and Bolton Wanderers

265. Tottenham Hotspur, Newcastle United and Birmingham City

266. West Ham, Chelsea, Liverpool and Aston Villa

267. Savo Milosevic

268. Yossi Benayoun

269. Matt Le Tissier, Dion Dublin, Roque Santa Cruz and Dwight Yorke

270. Mark Robins

Round 19

271.   Who has scored goals for the most different teams in the Premier League? A total of 7 different clubs.

272.   Which goalkeeper has kept the most clean sheets since the beginning of the Premier League?

273.   Which away player received a standing ovation at Goodison Park, when catching a cross into the opponent's penalty box with his hands when the Everton goalkeeper was injured? This game was played in December 2000.

274.   Who was the first Italian to play in the Premier League?

275.   Which Ghanaian player scored 24 Premier League goals for Leeds United between 1994-1997?

276.   Who was the Honduran left back to score from his own half for Wigan Athletic against Stoke City?

277.   A player missed a penalty and scored two own goals in a game against Chelsea. Can you name the player?

278.   Which player captained Blackburn Rovers to their first and only Premier League title in the season 1994-1995?

279.   Which Middlesbrough player scored a hat-trick in the 8-1 victory against Manchester City in May 2008?

280.   Can you name the three players who have received a record 8 red cards?

281.   What club did Louis Saha make his first Premier League appearance for?

282.   Who was the first midfielder to score 100 Premier League goals?

283. Which player scored a goal after his shot deflected off a beach ball in a game against Liverpool?

284. Who is the only player to have scored a hat-trick for three different Premier League teams?

285. Which player has the most Premier League assists?

Round 19 Answers

271. Craig Bellamy

272. Petr Cech

273. Paulo Di Canio

274. Andrea Silenzi

275. Tony Yeboah

276. Maynor Figueroa

277. Jonathan Walters

278. Tim Sherwood

279. Alfonso Alves

280. Duncan Ferguson, Richard Dunne and Patrick Vieira

281. Newcastle United

282. Matt Le Tissier

283. Darren Bent

284. Nicolas Anelka

285. Ryan Giggs

Round 20

286. Who scored the first ever Premier League goal?

287. Who are the only two players to have scored a Premier League headed hat-trick?

288. Which Arsenal player scored the only goal of the game when Arsenal beat Manchester United 1-0 at old Trafford in the 2001/2002 season? Arsenal secured the Premier League title after winning this game at Old Trafford.

289. Which player has played for more Premier League clubs than any other player?

290. Which player has scored the most Premier League goals from outside the box?

291. Who was the top goal scorer in the first Premier League season of 1992-1993?

292. Which player scored the 20,000th Premier League goal?

293. Who has scored the most own goals in the Premier League?

294. Who is the only player to score five goals in one half in Premier League history?

295. Who is the youngest ever scorer in the Premier League? Scoring when he was 16 years and 270 days old.

296. Who scored the fastest ever Premier League goal? The goal was scored after 8 seconds.

297. How many goalkeepers have scored a goal for their team in the Premier League?

298. Which goalkeeper has saved the most penalties in the Premier League?

299. Which player has made the most consecutive appearances in the Premier League? A total amount of 310.

300. Who was the oldest ever player to make an appearance in the Premier League? At an age of 43 years and 162 days.

Round 20 Answers

286.   Brian Deane

287.   Duncan Ferguson and Salomón Rondón

288.   Sylvain Wiltord

289.   Marcus Bent

290.   Frank Lampard

291.   Teddy Sheringham

292.   Mark Albrighton

293.   Richard Dunne

294.   Jermaine Defoe

295.   James Vaughan

296.   Shane Long

297.   Five

298.   David James

299.   Brad Friedel

300.   John Burridge

Congratulations!

You have completed all 20 rounds of the English Premier League Players Quiz Book.

There will be more quiz books coming your way soon by QuizGuy, so please keep this in mind.

One last thing………

If you have enjoyed the quiz book, please write a review on Amazon. This is helpful for the author and it will provide useful feedback.

Printed in Great Britain
by Amazon

51401413R00040